The CELEBRATE FAMILY Book

Your Family
Photo Here

You and Your Special, Wonderful,
One-of-a-Kind Family

by Ellen Sabin

and _____

WRITE YOUR NAME HERE

WATERING CAN® PRESS
www.wateringcanpress.com

WATERING CAN®

Growing Kids with Character

When you care about things and nurture them,
they will grow healthy, strong, and happy, and in turn,
they will make the world a better place.

All Watering Can Press titles are available at special quantity discounts for bulk purchases
for sales promotion, premiums, fund-raising, educational, or institutional use.

Watering Can Press offers customized versions of this book and will adjust content for use
by nonprofits and corporations in support of their community outreach and marketing goals.

**To inquire about bulk discounts or to learn more about customized book runs,
please visit our Web site or e-mail info@wateringcanpress.com.**

Text and illustrations © 2017 by Ellen Sabin
WATERING CAN is a registered trademark of Ellen Sabin.
Watering Can, New York, NY
Printed in China in December 2017

Written by Ellen Sabin
Illustrated by Kerren Barbas
Designed by Elynn Cohen

ISBN: 978-0-9826416-2-0

Web site address: www.wateringcanpress.com

Dear _____ ,

Because you are part of an amazing family, I am giving you this **CELEBRATE FAMILY BOOK**.

We all have families, and every family is unique.

In this book, you'll get to think about the people in your family and the ways that they are special to you. You'll find activities that let you get to know them better, create fun times together, and bring you closer to them, so you can enjoy your family even more. There are also ideas for ways to get through life's ups and downs with them and pages to record your favorite family memories.

Along the way, you'll discover that you are a very important part of your family!

I hope this book will help you enjoy exploring all the reasons you have to celebrate you and your one-of-a-kind, special family!

From, _____

Some "thank-yous"

- To MY family! I feel lucky every day—and in so many ways—that I had the fortune of growing up in a family full of inspiring, good, kind, loving, and giving people. Thank you, thank you, thank you, ALL, for being in my heart forever.

- There were many professionals—therapists, educators, adoption specialists, diversity and inclusion executives, family counselors—who contributed their time, expertise, and support. I especially want to thank the parents, caregivers, and children whose input helped shape, balance, and refine these pages.

- Heartfelt appreciation to the Morter Olson family. They've exemplified the values shared in this book and touched many lives by sharing their home, love, and family. Their philanthropic commitment to children propelled this book forward. I am honored to call them friends.

A NOTE TO ADULTS

This book is meant to inspire children to understand and respect that every family is unique and to find value, safety, joy, and pride in their own family.

It invites kids and families to practice the art of creating, enjoying, and celebrating good times, as well as facing and negotiating family challenges that arise along the way.

In turn, this book encourages children to express their range of feelings— from hope and joy, to confusion or frustration. Adults can be mindful, open, and responsive to support the conversation.

Even if children have the skills to read this book independently, it's fun and valuable for you to read through the book with them.

Ultimately, I hope The CELEBRATE FAMILY BOOK journey will help inspire children to form positive and character-building habits that will serve them in their relationships with family, friends, and community throughout their lives.

Table of Contents

What is The CELEBRATE FAMILY BOOK?

Welcome to Your CELEBRATE FAMILY BOOK!

This book is about YOU and all the wonderful, unique, awesome, silly, quirky, challenging, and remarkable things that make your family…YOUR FAMILY!

Think about it. There is no other family in the whole world that is just like yours.

That makes your family an incredibly special, irreplaceable, one-of-a-kind treasure.

And, after all, people always like treasures.

☆ So let's celebrate your family. ☆

What are you waiting for? Turn the page and get started! ● ● ● ➤

How does THE CELEBRATE FAMILY BOOK work?

First — You think about family: what it is and why it is so important.

Next — You get to write about your one-of-a-kind family and all the things that make it unique and special.

Then — You explore the ins and outs of family life so you and your family can enjoy the good times and help one another through any hard times.

And — Along the way, you will learn more about your family members, which will give you even more to celebrate! You'll also get to look at your own special value within your family that makes it complete.

Then — You get to spend time remembering special family moments. By writing them down, you can create a scrapbook to keep and cherish your favorite family memories forever.

Remember:

This is YOUR book, and you can use it however YOU want!

You can write in it, fill in the blanks, draw pictures, make a journal, and keep track of all the reasons you have to celebrate you and your family.

You don't have to do it all at once. You can read it and write in it as much as you want, and then put it away when you feel like it. Then, you can take it out again in a few days, weeks, or months and pick up where you left off.

You can use this book on your own sometimes, but it's much more fun if you share it with your family.

So, take your time and use your
CELEBRATE FAMILY BOOK
whenever and however you want!

What Makes a Family?

A family includes you and the people who love you, care for you, and support you.

They are the people who joke with you; laugh or cry with you;
fight and make up with you; and share, learn, play,
and grow with you.

Families are made of bonds that link them together for life.

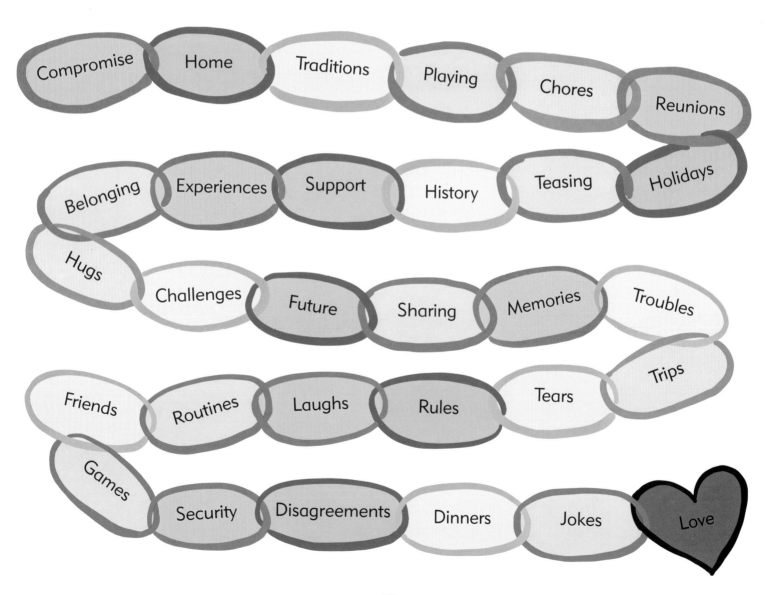

Compromise · Home · Traditions · Playing · Chores · Reunions

Belonging · Experiences · Support · History · Teasing · Holidays

Hugs · Challenges · Future · Sharing · Memories · Troubles

Friends · Routines · Laughs · Rules · Tears · Trips

Games · Security · Disagreements · Dinners · Jokes · Love

There are Many Kinds of Families

Families are like jigsaw puzzles! Each family member is a unique and important piece, and the pieces fit together to make a one-of-a-kind family.

In some families, kids live with a mom and dad, and in others they live with only one parent, or with two moms or two dads. Kids can also live with other relatives, like grandparents or aunts and uncles.

Sometimes kids are adopted and become part of new families or live with foster families.

Many kids have one home, and many others have parents who are divorced, so they may have two homes.

Some families are big with lots of children, cousins, and relatives. Others are small and made up of two people.

Some families live together or close to one another, while others live apart.

In some families, everyone shares the same race or religion. In others, family members come from all over the world and have many different backgrounds.

Families are made up in all sorts of different ways. The important part is that they fit together!

aunt

stepdad

brother

nephew

mom

stepsister

half brother

YOU!

godparent

cousin

uncle

dad

friend

adopted brother

niece

foster sister

great grandpa

Draw a Picture of Your Family

Below, draw a picture or paste a photo of you and your family.

Defining Family

People define "family" in different ways, but no matter
what words they use, family is a huge part of people's lives.

We asked some people about how they would define "family," and here's what they said:

Family is when my dad shows up for every soccer game or when my mom wakes up at 6:30 a.m. to walk me to the bus.

Sometimes my little brother bugs me, and sometimes it's hard when my dad is away. I don't think my family is perfect all the time, but I'm still glad that they're mine.

People in a family always have one another's backs.

I don't get to see some members of my family all the time, but I know that they love me, even when we're far apart.

My friends have families that are very different from mine. What makes us all the same is that we're lucky to have people who love, support, and take care of us.

I learned that the word "adopt" means to choose something as your own. My parents adopted me so we could be a family forever.

What Family Means to You

Talk to your family and ask everyone to write down what being part of the family means to them.

Don't forget to add your definition, too!

Your One-of-a-Kind Family

Did you know that no two snowflakes are exactly alike?

They are all beautiful and special.

They are all different in some ways.

You and your family are like snowflakes: beautiful, special, unique, and different from any other family.

Turn the page and start thinking about your own special family!

The Basics

My name is _____. I am _____ years old.

The people in my family are:

Name	Relationship to me	Age

Family Tree

A family tree shows the people who make up your family. It can include family members who are alive today as well as your relatives who lived long ago.

Ask an adult to help you fill in your tree and tell you a story about any relative who you don't know.

Remember, since every family is unique, your tree might have lots of extra branches. You may have important people to add like stepparents, aunts and uncles, foster or birth parents, or favorite cousins. Add in the special people who make up your family to complete your one-of-a-kind tree. If you don't know parts of your family history, that's OK. Fill in what you can.

Personalities

A personality is made up of the characteristics and qualities that make a person unique and different from other people.

Think of two people in your family. They are _____ and _____.

Person 1   Person 2

Circle the top three words that best describe Person 1, and put a square around the top three words that describe Person 2.

angry   **silly**   loud   **sad**   caring   polite

funny   FRIENDLY   LAZY   irritable

messy   sweet   **stylish**   shy   **casual**

stressed   WARM   smart   *loving*

serious   **honest**   **artistic**   hardworking

busy   quiet   goofy   carefree   ATHLETIC   kind

grumpy   gentle   happy

creative   proud   calm   brave   WORRIED

Now ask someone in your family to come up with five words about you, and write them here:

Introducing...Your Parents!

Pretend you are watching a movie about your mom, dad, or another special adult in your family.

Write down some things about this person that might be featured in a movie about his or her life. Where does he or she live or work? What are his or her favorite things to do? Who does this person like talking to and spending time with? If you can't think of anything, you can make up a story and make this person the main character.

Family Heroes

A hero is someone you look up to, someone you can learn from, and someone who has qualities you would like to have.

Heroes can be people you admire because they are caring, hardworking, smart, courageous, kind, or have other great qualities. These people can be your heroes for the things that you see them do, the way they act, or the way they make your life special.

Who are some of your family heroes?

Family member:

_____

What do you admire about
this person?

_____

_____

_____

Family member:

_____

What do you admire about
this person?

_____

_____

_____

Family member:

_____

What do you admire about
this person?

_____

_____

_____

Family member:

_____

What do you admire about
this person?

_____

_____

_____

Family Fun

What are your favorite things to do with your family?

Draw a picture of one of those things here.

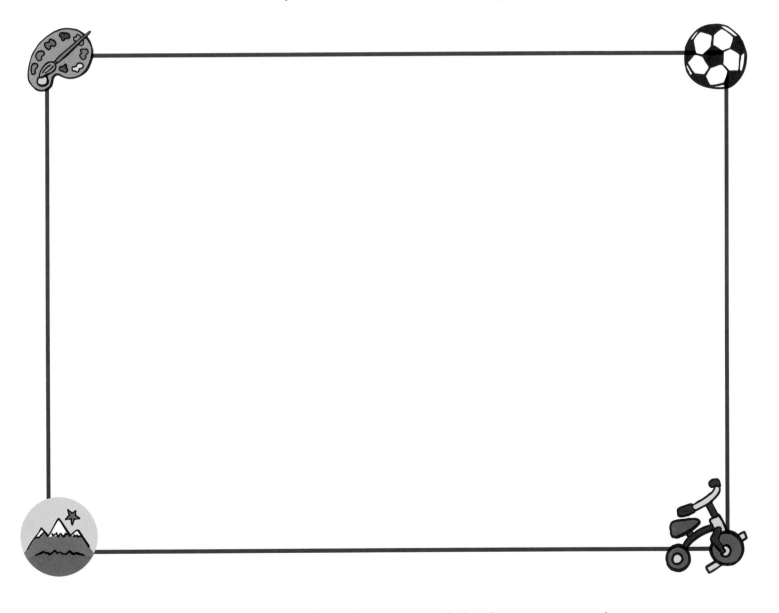

Spending time with your family is one of the best ways to bring you closer and make memories that will last forever.

Family Traditions

All families have special ways that they do things—traditions.

In your family, maybe you celebrate holidays in the same way every year or you often visit a favorite place. Maybe you have a regular game or TV night. Does your family get together for reunions or have special ways to honor your heritage? Perhaps every weekend you have a routine together or share a special meal.

Write down some of your family traditions.

Other Cool Family Stuff

My favorite meal with my family is

....

....

....

....

....

....

Describe where you live and what you like best about it.

....

....

....

....

One of my favorite relatives is

....

because ....

....

....

I have a pet ....

named ....

If you don't have a pet, what kind of animal do you like best?

....

....

My favorite holiday is

....

because ....

....

....

People in the same family are often similar.

No one is just like you, but you can probably think of some ways that you are like your family members. Maybe you look alike, have the same sense of humor or style, share favorite hobbies, or act the same in certain ways.

I am like .... in these ways:
(family member name here)

....

....

....

How are you different?

People in a family can also look different and act differently from one another in lots of ways. We all have different talents, feelings, experiences, and more.

I am different from .... in these ways:
(family member name here)

....

....

....

Questions About My Family

Are there things you would like to know about your family?

Maybe you are curious about what countries your ancestors came from, how your name was chosen for you, where your parents met, or other family facts. Perhaps you wonder about certain family situations. For example, if you were adopted or there was a divorce in your family, you might have questions about those things.

Write your questions here.

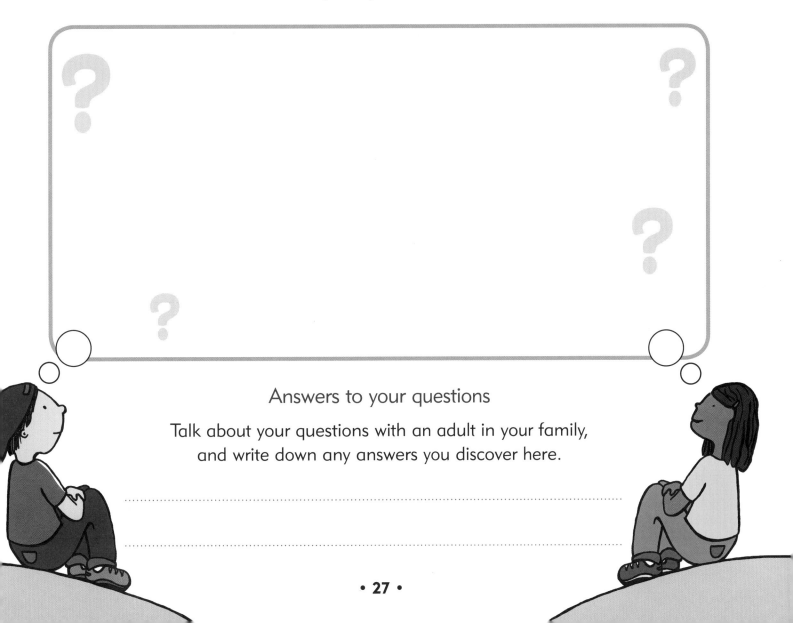

Answers to your questions

Talk about your questions with an adult in your family, and write down any answers you discover here.

Know Your Family

The better you know the people in your family, the closer you can be.

You probably know a lot about your family members already,
but there's always more to learn.

Do you know their favorite or least favorite...

Foods

Places

Books

Hobbies

Sports

Colors

Seasons

Jobs

TV shows

Animals

Jokes

Games

Stores

Subjects in school

Use this page to write down some of one another's likes and dislikes. If you don't know, just ask, and you'll get to find out new and interesting things about the people in your family.

Name: ....

Likes	Dislikes

Name: ....

Likes	Dislikes

Name: ....

Likes	Dislikes

Name: ....

Likes	Dislikes

YOU Are a Very Important Part of Your Family!

In fact, you are essential.

That means your family would not be the same without you. It would be incomplete. Your family needs you and loves you and all the wonderful and special things that make you . . . you!

Ask family members to tell you some of their favorite things about you and write them down here.

Did you know that no two people in the world have the exact same fingerprint?

You are one of a kind!

Ask an adult to help you stamp your fingerprint in the box below.

Let's Celebrate YOU

I'm proud of myself when I:

....

....

....

....

What I like best about myself is:

....

....

....

....

Some things I'm really good at are:

....

....

....

Some quirky things that make me unique are:

....

....

....

....

Wow! Your family is lucky to have you!

Celebrate Family with Compliments

Everyone likes hearing nice things from others, especially from the people who know them best!

On this page, you and your family members can fill in the balloons with compliments that you'd like to give one another.

Your Family Crest

In ancient times, knights and nobles often had symbols that represented their families. These were called crests.

A crest usually had certain parts, including a shield with a favorite background color or pattern as well as a main picture or symbols in the center to showcase things that were important to the family. Families often wrote a motto, or saying, at the bottom of the shield with words like "courage," "justice," or "love" that described the families' values and made them feel proud.

If your family had a crest, what would it look like?

Draw yours here.

FAMILY LIFE

Understanding, Enjoying, and Growing Together

Being part of a family means a lot of things.

Living as a family means looking out for one another,
respecting one another, and being kind to one another.

It also means sharing, compromising, helping out, and talking to one
another when things are good, or even when things are upsetting.

Sometimes family life is easy, and sometimes there can be challenges.

That's because families go through a lot together.
They can have good times together, face changes together,
and can also get through hard times together.

In this chapter, you get to think more about your family
and ways to enjoy one another and stick together
to make family life the best it can be.

Quality Time

Families spend time together doing lots of different things.
Whether you read books, play sports, eat dinners, or just hang out,
quality time with your family is important.

Draw a picture of something that you and your family do together that makes you happy.

Sometimes people get busy, aren't around, or forget to share family time.
You can fill in these coupons to remind a family member how much you enjoy spending
time with him or her. And don't forget that your family wants time with you, too!

Quality Time COUPON

To: .... From: ....
This coupon is for one-on-one time
for us to ....

....
(Write something you enjoy doing
with that person here.)

Quality Time COUPON

To: .... From: ....
This coupon is for one-on-one time
for us to ....

....
(Write something you enjoy doing
with that person here.)

Make Family F U N

Trying and doing new things is always fun, especially with people in your family.

TO DO:
Make a list of things you want to do in the future with someone in your family.

Warm Fuzzies

Write down some things that someone in your family does that make you feel happy and warm inside.

Getting Along

Living with family means sharing time, space, things, and people. It's not always easy to share. That's one reason why families might not get along perfectly all the time. That's normal.

One of the best ways to get along with your family is to remember to do your part and treat them how you like to be treated.

How do YOU like to be treated?

I hope that my family members will: (circle all that apply)

treat me nicely · be respectful of my things

enjoy quality time with me · notice if I feel sad or hurt · **BE PATIENT** · protect me from things that could hurt me

say "sorry" · share with me · give me attention

APPRECIATE ME

ENCOURAGE ME TO BE MY BEST · say "please" and "thank you"

stand up for me · tell me when they're proud of me

You probably circled all of them!

That means you hope others will take the time to understand you, be kind to you, and take care of you. Well, just remember that the people in your family also want the same things from you!

Talk to your family about other things that you can all do to get along.

Challenges

Families face life together. That means that, along with all the good times, sometimes family members have days when they are upset with one another or upset about other things. People we love can do things that upset us. It's OK if you sometimes feel mad at someone in your family.

Through life's challenges, it helps to talk things out, remember that family loves you, and find positive ways to feel better when you are down.

Family members are often the people who can help you get through tough times.

There are also things that YOU can do that might make you feel better when you're upset.

Here are some ideas:

Take deep breaths

Play with your pet

Listen to music

Sleep enough and eat well

Go for a walk or run

Play outside

Talk to a counselor

Visit a friend

Do something nice for others

Read a book

Find a peaceful place

Talk to family members

Change

Change is a natural part of life. It happens all the time. As people have new experiences, they are constantly growing and changing.

▶ Some changes are exciting and we look forward to them, like summer vacation.

▶ Some changes can feel bad at first but then feel better, like when you start at a new school. In the beginning you don't know anyone, but before you know it, you've made new friends.

▶ Some changes happen naturally, like when a tree loses leaves or grows flowers. Others happen because we work on them, like how you get smarter when you study at school.

▶ And some changes happen that we don't expect and take us by surprise.

How have you changed?

How tall were you last year? _____ How tall are you today? _____

What is your favorite sport or hobby? _____
As you practice, you get better and better. That's a good change.

You probably enjoy different things today than when you were younger. What was your favorite game or toy when you were five years old? _____
What is it today? _____

Every day you learn new things in school. How much you know keeps changing as you learn more and more!

How many teeth have you lost? _____ When you lose your baby teeth, your smile looks different, and that's a change. Then your smile changes again when your new teeth grow in.

Because a family is made up of people who are connected to one another, whenever one person in a family has a big change, it can affect everyone else. So change is also a natural and normal part of family life.

Sometimes a new baby is born or a family grows if a new sibling is adopted or if stepsiblings move in together. Other times, family members take long trips or move away. Families change when someone gets married or divorced. They also change when a family member dies.

Families sometimes move. Adults can change jobs. Kids may change schools. Family members get older, find new hobbies, make new friends, and have new experiences.

Write about any changes in your family life.
What about these changes made you happy? What was hard about them?

It might make you feel better to know that even when there are changes in a family, many things remain the same.

Helping Hands

Family is often the people who lend a hand and support you in your life.

When I feel sad, the person I talk to is:

....

When I'm sick, this person always takes care of me:

....

When I need help with homework, I can count on:

....

When I'm frustrated or confused, I get good advice from:

....

When I feel scared, I can call or text people. Their names are:

....

....

....

You have lots of people who support you. Besides family, there are teachers, coaches, and other trusted adults. You should always ask for help when you need it.

Family Wishes

Everyone has hopes, dreams, and wishes for the future. Family members often cheer for one another and then celebrate together when wishes come true.

Get together with your family and create a "Family Wishes" wall. Here's how:

3. Hang your stars— your dreams and wishes—on the wall at home.

1. Take several big pieces of paper and cut them into the shape of stars.

2. On each star, write your wishes for yourself, for someone in your family, or a wish for the whole family.

Then you can see everyone's wishes on the wall and be one step closer to making them come true!

Pitching In

Have you ever noticed how much faster and easier it is to get something done when you have help? Well, there are lots of things to do to take care of a home and the people in it. And each member of a family is important and can help around the home.

Jobs or chores I often do include: ....

....

....

There are probably some jobs that you are really good at doing and others that you don't enjoy as much. It's great that you can do your part to help out!

Your parents have a lot to do to keep your family and home running smoothly, too!

✔ Make meals
✔ Do laundry
✔ Earn money
✔ Drive you places
✔ Help you with homework

✔ Hug you
✔ Care for you when you are sick
✔ Take care of pets
✔ Clean the house
✔ . . . SO much more

Wow, that's a LOT! Now would be the perfect time to take a break from your book and say a big THANK-YOU to them for all they do to take care of you, your home, and your family.

Write a Letter to YOU

Being a parent and caregiver can be amazing, but it's not always easy.

On this page, you can write a note to your future self so you can remember some things you may want to do (or not do) when you are a mom or dad.

Dear me (of the future),

_____

_____

_____

_____

_____

_____

_____

_____

From, _____

Home Sweet Home

Whether you live in a house or an apartment, in the city or the country, or in a place that's big or small, your home is a special place.

That's because home, no matter how long you've lived there, is where you can always go to be with your family.

Here's a maze that will remind you that you can always find your way home to family!

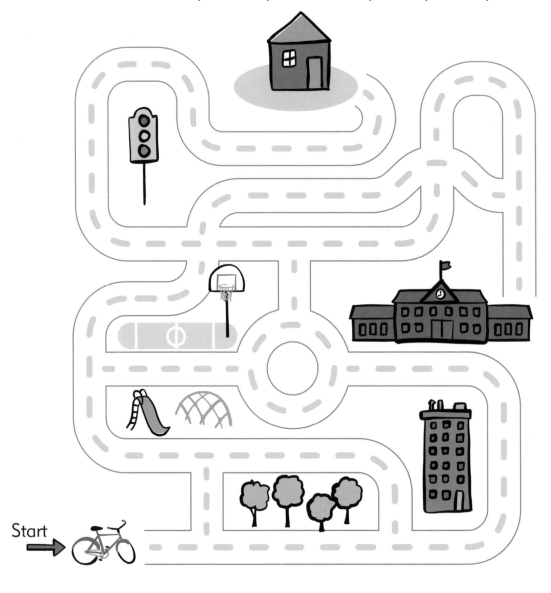

Certificates

. . . to be shared with family!

A Note of Thanks

To _ _ _ _ _ _ _ _ _ From _ _ _ _ _ _ _ _ _ _

I want to thank you for _ _ _ _ _ _ _ _ _ _ _ _

I appreciate you and all the nice things you do!

A Gift of Sharing

To_ _ _ _ _ _ _ _ _ _ _ From _ _ _ _ _ _ _ _ _ _

I know that you like my _ _ _ _ _ _ _ _ _ _ _

This certificate gives you permission to borrow it today. I hope you enjoy it.

A Comforting Note

To_ _ _ _ _ _ _ _ _ _ From _ _ _ _ _ _ _ _ _ _

This note entitles you to a hug, cuddle, or shoulder to lean on if you want to talk.

I hope you feel my love whenever you are feeling down.

I Support You

To _ _ _ _ _ _ _ _ _ _ From _ _ _ _ _ _ _ _ _ _

If there is a day when you need me to do something or you want my help, please ask for it. This certificate means I will lend you a hand.

Being Thankful

Families share lots of experiences together: fun times, ups and downs, changes, and more. Through it all, it's great to get in the habit of thinking about the positive parts of these experiences and the many reasons you have to be thankful.

Here you can list some things that you are thankful for about your family. They can be big things—like being thankful for your home—and little things— like being thankful for the delicious dinner you had last night.

Come back to this page often, and you'll find that there's always something new to be thankful for!

From Family to Friends and Community

Your family is your first and closest community. It's also one of the places where you get the best practice in getting along with friends and other people.

Think about your family as if it were a plant. It needs to be nurtured to help it grow strong and healthy.

When you use your skills at being . . .

helpful

thankful

compromising

respectful

communicative

accepting

. . . you are doing your part in giving your family water and sun to keep it growing happy and healthy.

You can use those same skills to help build strong and lasting friendships, too!

Your Family Scrapbook

No matter where the road of your
life takes you, your family will be with
you because you carry them in your heart
and in your memories. Family is forever.

Turn the page to make a scrapbook that will help you
always remember your favorite family times.

Family Stories

Every family has special stories about the past.

Some stories might be about relatives who lived a long time ago or whom you never met. Others might be about things that happened to someone in your family before you were born. Stories might also be about times that you remember and like to hear retold.

Here you can write down one of your favorite family stories.

Picture Perfect

On this page, attach some of your favorite family pictures.

Whenever you want to smile, you can return to this page and think of these people or remember these happy times.

A special day

A family trip or holiday

An old picture of your relatives or a picture of you as a baby

Your family today!

Special Memories

You've probably had a lot of special moments with people in your family.

You can write about some of those times here.

A happy memory

....

....

....

A funny moment

....

....

....

A secret you shared

....

....

....

A family adventure

....

....

....

Vacation Memories

What's the best trip you and your family have ever been on together?

Use this page to write about your favorite family vacation. If you can't think of one, you can make up a story about a trip you'd like to take one day.

Words of Wisdom

Sometimes the best advice you can ever
get is from the people in your family.

Write down some things that family members have taught you
that you think will be worth remembering in the years ahead.

Keep Family in Your Heart

Is there someone in your family who you miss because they are no longer around to spend time with you?

If a family member moved away or died, or if you can't see them for other reasons, you can still remember them. One way to keep that person close to your heart is to think about him or her. Paste or draw a picture of that person here.

Sometimes we wish we could have said a few last things to people before they're gone.

Maybe you wish you could say "I love you" one more time. Maybe you feel hurt and want to tell them why. If you could talk to this person now, what would you say?

Capture Some History

Grab a pencil and imagine that you are a reporter. Sit down with a parent, grandparent, or other adult in your family, and write down their responses to the questions below.

The News

SUNDAY, MARCH 26

VOL. III, NUMBER IV

When you were my age, what were your favorite things to do?

....

....

....

What was your favorite subject in school?

....

....

....

Tell me about the place where you grew up.

....

....

....

....

What were your parents like?

....

....

....

....

....

What advice can you give me about family?

....

....

....

....

....

Time Capsule

A time capsule is a container that keeps things from history so they can be discovered at a later time in the future. Usually time capsules are buried and then found by someone else. This one gets to be yours to rediscover whenever you open this page.

Fill this page with items that you want to remember and perhaps even pass down to your children in the future.

Family Recipe

Family Picture

Find your favorite family photo to frame and keep.

Childhood Stuff

Lots of people have blankets, stuffed animals, or books from their childhood that they like to keep forever. What was your favorite childhood item? ....

Family Treasure

Is there a piece of jewelry, art, or another trinket that you or others might want to share with future family members?

Birthday Reminders

Write down the birthdays of your family members. That way you'll remember to wish them a happy birthday every year on their special day!

OTHER STUFF

YAY YOU!

Congratulations!

This CELEBRATE FAMILY BOOK certificate shows that you take time to appreciate and understand your family and that you do your best to help keep it close and strong.

THE CELEBRATE FAMILY BOOK

This certificate is awarded to

#1

....

WRITE YOUR NAME HERE

for being an important part of
a special family!

....

DATE

Now that you know how great it feels to celebrate family, keep it up! Always remember how special they are, how important you are to them, and that your one-of-a-kind family is yours forever.

Join Watering Can® Press in growing kids with character.

www.wateringcanpress.com

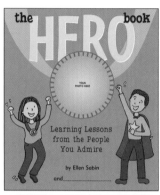

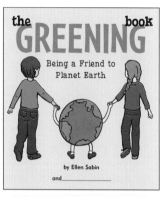

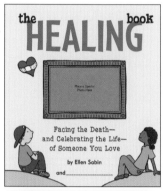

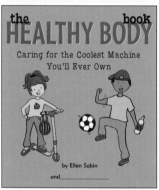

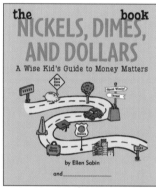

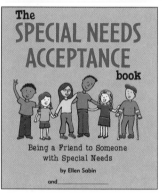

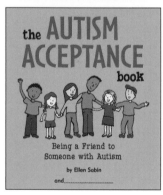

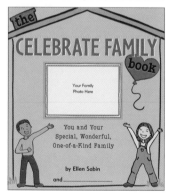

- Find and order other Watering Can® books.
- Take advantage of bulk discounts for schools and organizations.
- Learn about customizing our books for corporate and community outreach.
- View the **FREE** Teacher's Guides and Parent's Guides available on our site.

We hope you've explored a lot
about yourself and
your amazing family.
We also hope that you have learned
new ways to enjoy, honor,
and celebrate family now and forever.